CASH
MANAGEMENT
stewardship of the church's cash resources

by Manfred Holck Jr.

Augsburg Publishing House
Minneapolis, Minnesota

ADMINISTRATION SERIES FOR CHURCHES

Topics in this series are grouped in seven major areas: Theology of Administration; Organization Development; Finance, Accounting and Cash Control; Program Planning and Evaluation; Personnel and Office Policies; Property and Insurance; Communications. Each publication in this series will have been field-tested in congregations and presented by authoritative writers. Topic suggestions and comments are sought from all readers.

John R. Dewey
Division for Life and Mission in the Congregation
The American Lutheran Church

Cash Management

CONTENTS

Church Cash Management 4

Using Church Cash Management 7
   Some Opportunities to Utilize Cash Flow 8
   Cash Management and Budgets 8
   The Stewardship of Management 9

Receiving, Counting, and Recording the Offering 11
   Procedures 12
   Steps in the Counting Process 13

Accounting Procedures and Cash Management 16
   Basic Accounting Systems Principles 17
   Journals and Ledgers 18
   Bank Statement Reconciliation 22
   The Financial Statements 23
   The Cash Flow Forecast 23
   Maximizing Cash Through Proper Spending 26

How to Invest Surplus Cash 31
   Investment Vehicles for Cash 31
   A Word of Caution 32
   Special Funds and Their Investment 33
   Interfund Borrowings 34
   Other Cash Management Opportunities 35
   Handling Benevolence Monies 36

In Support of the Mission of the Church 37

Bibliography 39

Illustrations
  1. Weekly Offering Count Sheet 14
  2. Monthly Offering Report 15
  3. Monthly Report of Offerings to Church Council 15
  4. Cash Receipts Journal 19
  5. Cash Disbursements Journal 20
  6. Selected General Ledger Accounts 21
  7. Trial Balance and Work Sheet 24
  8. Financial Statements 25
  9. Cash Forecast Worksheet 28
  10. Flow Chart—Offerings 29
  11. Flow Chart—Disbursements 30

Church
cash
management

A church council member once told me that the trouble with churches is that they never make a profit. Successful congregations, said this enlightened businessman, are those that can build up a comfortable surplus. After all, when hard times come, a surplus is needed to insure the congregation against financial disaster. That only makes good business sense!

But the church is neither in the business of declaring cash dividends nor of saving money or generating a surplus. Its business is mission and ministry. Yet, far too many lay leaders judge the success of a congregation only by the size of its bankbook. Get all you can, spend as little as you must, save the rest, and the congregation will succeed, they contend.

Cash rich congregations may indeed go on for a long time spending their money on salaries and building maintenance. However, merely perpetuating an institution is not the purpose of the church. Mission and ministry is. Using cash to help people fulfill mission and ministry is the ideal to be achieved, whether the dollars are few or many. Pastors must be paid and buildings must be maintained, to be sure, for that work to be done. But then, it is not only a maintenance arrangement. Indeed cash rich congregations can be an active source of talent and money for achieving the church's mission.

On the other hand, cash poor congregations are not necessarily unsuccessful. They may indeed be furthering the cause of the kingdom far more than anyone realizes, always spending dollars received for programs helpful to people. By allocating their resources effectively, they may indeed be far more successful at fulfilling the mission of the church than those congregations with cash-filled coffers. Of course, congregations can squander their resources, too.

4

Nevertheless, no matter how much your own congregation may now have in its bank account, cash management, that is, the proper management and the utilization of the congregation's resources, is an ongoing and persistent concern for church leaders. The amount of money is not as important as the use of it to maximize the available funds. Effective cash management seeks precisely that goal no matter what the dollar amount involved.

Managing congregational cash, however, is not always done effectively or purposefully or knowledgeably. In today's economy, congregations that fail to maximize resources may be unintentionally squandering the congregation's money. Many services the church offers are increasing in cost. Unless leaders are managing costs through adequate controls and spending safeguards, they are simply wasting resources, reneging on their stewardship responsibilities to the membership.

The pressure on congregational leaders to maximize the use of every single dollar given is tremendous. Not all leaders may recognize that responsibility equally, but it is there, nevertheless. Unless those leaders seek out the best methods possible to fulfill their responsibilities, they are like the one talent man in our Lord's parable of the talents—"wicked and slothful!"

The church has always been under pressure to use its resources wisely. Even now, as inflation eats away at the purchasing power of every dollar given, as energy costs use more and more of those dollars given, it is imperative that lay leaders seek out every possible procedure for maximizing effective cash flow.

The giving habits of members in most congregations haven't changed much. Vacations take an annual summer toll of offerings and the holiday season brings its own greater response. Month by month bills keep coming in. Sometimes there is not enough money to meet them, sometimes more than enough. People are not likely to change and the offering pattern will inevitably curve down in summer and up in winter. Thus exceptional management skills are required to make those surplus dollars at the peaks extend across the valleys. Weekends on the lake or the beach preempt weekends in the church—while the salaries, and the utilities, and benevolences are still to be paid. The pressures never cease to make ends meet in the church, no less than at home.

Congregations, therefore, have been asking for help in managing their money. That is the purpose of this booklet, to offer specific suggestions on how (1) to stretch congregational dollars even more, (2) to make the offering do more than seems possible, and (3) to assist leaders to carry out the trust responsibilities of their stewardship of the church's resources.

Congregational leaders generally agree that adequate cash management techniques are extremely important today.

But what is cash management in the church?

Cash management is not only the process of investing surplus money at the highest possible yield rate. It also involves every facet of cash handling procedure from proper methods for counting the offering, to accounting for the receipt and disbursement of funds. It includes investing at the highest yield

5

relative to safety required, the spending of cash, and generally to control the flow of cash in effective ways to make the best possible use of it.

Thus, this booklet presumes the following about church cash management:

1. Cash management is not merely the process of safeguarding church funds. It is the careful use of a congregation's cash resources in order to accomplish a more effective ministry.

2. Church budgets (see the booklet, *Annual Budgeting*, in this series) deal with how funds are to be used. Church cash management is concerned with the conservation and increase of funds, the maximization of resources—stretching every dollar given to its maximum possible use.

3. Congregational resources are many. Among such resources are people, their talents, their time, and their money. The flow of that money through the staff and programs of the congregation is in itself as crucial a resource for ministry as the use of people, time, and talents.

4. The ultimate purpose of cash management (and the criteria for the suggestions in this booklet) is to make sure that whatever cash the congregation has available is always working toward the attainment of that congregation's goals for ministry. Effective church cash management puts cash to work for ministry as soon as possible.

5. A biblical model for church cash management is found in the parable of the talents (Matthew 25:14-30). Among other observations, the one talent man is admonished for not having invested "my money with the bankers, and at my coming I should have received what was my own with interest." It is not the size of the financial responsibility that makes the difference—it is the attitude of responsible stewardship that counts. To hoard the gifts which we are to manage for congregation and God is to render inert the living expressions of love from God's people.

Using
church cash
management

The benefits of proper church cash management are obvious: maximum utilization of cash funds, potentially higher income through various investments of idle cash, efficiency in programs as cash use is honed to greater efficiency.

Every congregation is involved in cash management. It has to be, whether it wants to be or not. Just having cash requires its use. Of course, in some places that management will be lazy, in others efficient. We all manage cash, including congregational lay leaders. Such management can have a direct bearing on both mission and ministry.

As the contents of this booklet are studied, it should be clear that there are many ways to manage cash. No matter which way of managing cash is chosen, it should maximize the use of that resource. As much as possible can then be accomplished for the mission and ministry of the church. Effective church cash management can stretch available dollars beyond that which becomes possible with "seat of the pants" cash management.

Church cash management also involves the investing of available cash. Here the problem is to achieve the greatest possible yield with the least amount of risk. Good church cash management can mean more cash resources from interest income.

Efficiencies in program implementation will also be evident when church cash management is resolutely pursued by congregational leaders. If cash is to be used efficiently, the program administrators must use their budget dollars as carefully as the treasurer searches out idle cash for investing.

Program leaders will consequently be forced to seek out the most effective way to achieve their goals consistent with maintenance of desired quality in the program and the funds available. They will estimate costs more precisely, spend money by the budget, and seek out the latest possible bill payment dates without additional credit costs. Conserving cash by planning programs carefully not only maximizes cash use but also can generate a more successful program. Cash management saves money that might otherwise be spent through careless planning.

Some Opportunities to Utilize Cash Flow

There are many opportunities for improving the handling of cash. It is important that congregational leaders are interested in ferreting out these possibilities. Readers can think of additional procedures, but a few are listed here.

Church cash management can be used effectively to flatten out the peaks and the valleys in monthly offerings. A cash flow plan will clearly show when cash can be expected and when expenses are due to be paid. Matching the two by anticipating the need is the basis for church cash management. Don't get carried away by the volume of April offerings or depressed by the lack of dollars in the summer. Planning ahead can hold up some dollars from the good times to meet the expenses of poorer times. Without planning, however, the optimism of December can put the congregation's costs in summer all out of kilter. Dollars put aside in peak times are used to meet the expenses of slow periods. That's church cash management, but not entirely a widespread practice. Yet this is perhaps the most obvious opportunity for practicing cash management.

A few congregations have endowment funds, the income of which is often designated for general congregational use. The investment of these funds provides another opportunity for utilizing a plan of church cash management. If as much income as possible is a goal for that fund, it must be managed well to achieve that objective.

Other funds accumulating for specific purposes, such as memorial funds or building funds, are also to be invested safely to achieve the highest possible yield. Such funds cannot be left to accumulate idly in the church's checking account. Money is put to work multiplying itself for specific programs until such time as funds are paid out for approved goods or services.

Cash Management and Budgets

The church budgeting process is the topic of another booklet in this series, and proper cash management is an essential part of that process. Budgets depend on the availability of cash funds. Programs depend on budgets. How cash is managed determines, in part, the availability of funds and the potentials possible for program spending. There are significant opportunities for using church cash management techniques successfully in the development of a congregation's budget spending plan.

Church cash management is not budgeting. The two processes are distinct. Cash management maximizes the use of cash *before* it is spent. Budgeting maximizes the way in which *available* cash is to be spent. A church budget defines how money is to be spent. Cash management seeks ways to conserve cash not yet needed for budgeted items—in fact utilizing available resources in the meantime to increase those funds.

The Stewardship of Management

Christian stewardship concepts insist upon adequate methods of church cash management. After all, those who are stewards have been placed in a trust relationship to those whose money they manage. Whatever assists in fulfilling that responsibility should be pursued. Cash management is a way by which stewardship responsibilities can be fulfilled. It would be imprudent for congregational leaders not to utilize the most effective and tested methods for maximizing the offerings given by the membership each week.

The parables of Jesus provide some clues to effective stewardship on the part of those who care for other people's gifts. The parable of the talents, Matthew 25:14-30, includes several elements that suggest the responsibility of caring for another's possessions.

The amounts entrusted to God's stewards will vary. Jesus makes this point quite definitely: one servant received five talents, one had two talents to work with, and one servant was given only one talent. It is instructive that the servants who received the five and two talent responsibilities did something about it. The caretaker of the one talent gift did nothing that might endanger or enhance his stewardship. In fact, there was only a rebuke for this lack of concern that brought a loss of interest for the master in the parable.

At this point it is wise not to press the rest of the parable. This is not a promise of a special blessing for carrying out our responsibility for the gifts of fellow Christians. The parable stands rather as a reminder that these treasures are not the steward's own, but that they are to be handled well for the Master. In the parallel parable of the pounds, Luke 19:11-26, our Lord makes much the same points.

In another more difficult parable, that of the dishonest steward, Luke 16:1-9, Jesus tells a story that casts some light on the utilization of the gift of wisdom. One might take the parable apart, excuse the steward as being the source of his master's wealth, and find all sorts of allegorical application. But perhaps it is better to begin with the closing observation of Jesus: "The master commended the dishonest steward for his shrewdness; for the sons of this world are more shrewd in dealing with their generation than the sons of light." There is a bite in these words—a bite that makes us read on: "He who is faithful in a very little is faithful also in much."

So in all three parables the reader is drawn back to the simple truth that even the modest responsibility toward the gifts handled for a parish remains a trust from God. The steward is asked to be faithful and wise in stewardship. This is no time to abdicate the wisdom and patience God gave for such a responsible task.

At this point the task of the church council, or of the committee dealing with the financial resources of the church, takes on a new dimension. It is possible that past patterns of handling offerings and paying bills have covered up better ways of serving God and the congregation. It is possible that now is the time to question, "Why do we do things that way?" It may even be possible that there really isn't much that can be done to make better use of the gifts of God's people—but no one can know until a step-by-step evaluation is done of the ways this, or any, congregation handles its cash.

Whatever can be done to improve church cash management is part of good stewardship. How well church leaders fulfill that responsibility is a measure of effective money management. By the nature of the stewardship a congregation confers on its leaders, they are expected to manage the financial life of the parish well. How this can be done is important.

The chapters to follow will explore various cash management methods for churches.

Receiving, counting, and recording the offering

Church cash management begins at the point where a gift is placed in the offering plate. From then on, how that money is handled will make a difference in how effective the management of cash in that congregation really is.

Cash management does not begin only when there happens to be a surplus of cash in the bank, it begins as soon as the coins, bills, or checks become an offering. The immediate steps are procedural, of course, and don't generate more money. They may save money by keeping the offering safe from prying hands, but they won't help the money multiply—not yet. Remember that one of the basic assumptions in cash management, previously noted, is that church cash management means not only saving funds but also safeguarding funds. How the offering is handled is determined by such safeguards (internal control) surrounding its collection, counting, recording, and depositing.

A basic principle of internal control for any accounting system is that of separation of duties between those who handle cash receipts and those who handle cash disbursements. The purpose of this control is to eliminate the potential problem of having someone divert money and cover up the act by making it appear the expense was appropriate. Those who have access to cash receipts *and* cash disbursements simply have an easier time stealing money.

That control by itself is insufficient to guarantee the safety of all money, but it is basic. It is a critical control with respect to assignment of responsibility for the offering once it is received. Other controls to safeguard the congregation's assets will be listed later.

Thus, whoever is assigned responsibility for counting the offering is not to be the same person who writes checks and pays the bills. Nor is the teller to be the person who makes entries into the cash receipts and cash disbursements journal, or one who records individual members contributions. In most congregations the division of responsibility works out something like this:

Treasurer—responsible for maintaining the financial records, and often, along with a second person, signing all checks.

Financial secretary—responsible for counting and depositing all money received.

Assistant financial secretary—responsible for recording contributions by individuals to their personal giving records.

Finance committee—responsible for securing personnel to count, record, and disburse funds, for developing the annual budget, for reconciling the bank statements, for cash management, and for total financial planning.

In the typical situation the financial secretary is responsible for making sure that all offerings are safely placed in the bank account. But the financial secretary does not do the job all alone. In fact, another principle of internal control related to church accounting is that at least two people always count the cash. To put it another way, it is not good control of cash to have only one person with access to the cash at any time.

The purpose of this control is to protect the cash and to protect those who count the cash. When two or more persons are required to be with the cash and count it, the likelihood of that cash being accurately counted is heightened. Two persons are less likely to make errors of count or judgment. Two people, working together, are less likely to cooperate in the theft of money.

Furthermore, requiring two people to be present with the cash at all times eliminates the suspicions that might be created toward only one person if anyone thinks some money is missing. This control protects the money and the people counting the money, too. It seems easier to volunteer when risks are reduced.

So, one person alone should not be asked to count the offering. Two or more must do the job. In many congregations, however, the same person has been counting offerings for twenty years with thanks from others that at least someone is willing to do the job. But it is a risky and unfair arrangement for all parties and should be corrected promptly.

When two or more persons are assigned the money counting task, some will object to a regular Sunday morning assignment since the task could interfere with family worship or Sunday dinner. Rotating counters will help. That policy offers the experience to others and counting is then not a burden on anyone. A coordinator plus an easy and efficient system makes the experience less burdensome.

Procedures

As soon as the service is ended, two persons assigned the task remove the offering plates from the altar. The church council should insist that two people go to the altar together to get the money. For right here is the first place where money can be lost unless proper controls are followed.

Both persons carry the money to the counting place. There, in a quiet, safe, well lighted room with ample tables, pencils, forms, and an adding machine the counting can begin promptly.

Some congregations, however, take the offering immediately to the bank and deposit it, uncounted, in the night depository. That's alright providing that on the next day, or soon thereafter, at least two people go to the bank, retrieve the bag, unlock it, and count the money there and then.

Control is thrown away if the money is put into the bank without counting and then the church secretary goes over on Monday morning to count it in a private, locked room at the bank! One person with an uncounted amount of money is in a situation full of potential trouble. And a friendly bank teller should not count the money either, alone, until a deposit slip has been prepared against which a count can be compared by that teller.

But the best place and the best time to count the Sunday morning offering (or any other offering for that matter) is immediately *after the service and at the church.* (Counting money does not replace worship.)

Steps in the Counting Process

The counting process can be facilitated by using appropriate forms and keeping the procedure as simple as possible. Suggested steps are these:

1. Separate all loose coins, bills, and checks from the offering envelopes. Prepare recording slips for checks not in envelopes to indicate donor, amount, and purpose.

2. Remove all coins, bills, and checks from the offering envelopes. Be certain the amount removed is correctly marked on the outside of each envelope. If discrepancies appear, mark amount enclosed on envelope and request the assistant financial secretary to notify donor.

3. Prepare adding machine tapes to verify the total of coins, bills, and checks removed from envelopes with totals marked on envelope.

4. Record various sources of coins, bills, and checks on a counting form.

5. Prepare deposit slip and verify total deposit with total coins, bills, and checks received. Distribute copies of deposit slip and counting form to treasurer and assistant financial secretary. Give all empty envelopes with supporting total tape to assistant financial secretary for recording to individual contributors' records.

6. At least two persons take the deposit bag with appropriate deposit slip to the bank for deposit.

The illustrated forms (1-3), which appear on the next pages, may be helpful in expediting the counting and recording of the offering.

ILLUSTRATION 1

Weekly Offering Count Sheet

Date_____

	Coins	Bills	Checks	Total	Fund Totals
Current Fund					
Envelopes	_____	_____	_____	_____	
Loose plate	_____	_____	_____	_____	_____
Building Fund					
Envelopes	_____	_____	_____	_____	
Loose plate	_____	_____	_____	_____	_____
Benevolences					
Envelopes	_____	_____	_____	_____	
Loose plate	_____	_____	_____	_____	_____
Memorials					
Envelopes	_____	_____	_____	_____	
Loose plate	_____	_____	_____	_____	_____
Other Funds					
Envelopes	_____	_____	_____	_____	
Loose plate	_____	_____	_____	_____	_____
Total Deposit	_____	_____	_____	_____	_____

Counted by:_____ Date_____

Counted by:_____ Date_____

Copies of this report to: Treasurer, Financial Secretary, Assistant Financial Secretary. Attach duplicate copy of deposit slip to original of this report for Treasurer.

ILLUSTRATION 2

Monthly Offering Report

Month_____

Year _____

	Week 1	Week 2	Week 3	Week 4	Week 5	Total
Current Fund						
Building Fund						
Benevolences						
Memorials						
Other Funds						
Total Deposit						

Financial Secretary_____ Date_____

Copies of this report to: Treasurer, Financial Secretary, Assistant Financial Secretary.

ILLUSTRATION 3

Monthly Report of Offerings to Church Council

	This Month			Year to Date			Annual Budget
	Budget	Actual	Year Ago	Budget	Actual	Year Ago	
Current							
Building							
Benevolences							
Memorials							
Other							
Total							

15

Accounting procedures and cash management

Church accounting systems are as numerous and as varied as are congregations. There simply has been no successful effort made for use of a standardized church accounting system. Congregations have been free to develop their own procedures and with each new treasurer the system has often been changed.

Systems have been suggested, of course. Many books on church finance have proposed systems espoused by the author. Each of those systems has had its distinct advantages.

However, too often the systems have been developed on the pattern of a business enterprise and so are not entirely appropriate for congregations. Since a congregation is not in the business of generating a profit or accumulating a surplus, reports that reveal net earnings or changes in net worth are not particularly helpful in understanding what has happened to a congregation's cash.

The most recent attempt by professional accountants to develop standard financial statements for congregations has been by the Accounting Standards Subcommittee on Nonprofit Organizations of the American Institute of Certified Public Accountants (AICPA). Their guide on accounting principles and reporting practices for nonprofit organizations, when published, will be the standard suggested for use by the accounting profession. It will be a help toward guiding congregations in the development of their own system compatible with others and understandable by their members. If this guide is not yet available, see the *Complete Handbook of Church Accounting*, which suggests several alternative church accounting systems. Also refer to the bibliography, pages 39-40, for additional suggestions.

Basic Accounting Systems Principles

There are, of course, certain concepts basic to any church accounting system.

1. It should be a double entry bookkeeping system.

Single entry systems are not uncommon, but the double entry system of debits (dr.) and credits (cr.) provides a check on mathematical accuracy and a certain compatibility with other systems that makes it superior to the single entry system.

In double entry bookkeeping every entry is made twice. Thus, when cash is received, it is debited to the cash account (because asset accounts normally have a debit balance) and credited to the income account. Money spent is credited to cash (the normal debit balance is reduced) and debited to an expense account. In every transaction a debit equals a credit. And the sum of all the debit entries during a period equals the sum of all the credit entries. That's the way the system works.

Mistakes can still be made, of course, because entries can be debited or credited to the wrong accounts and the debits will still equal the credits. But the chance of mathematical error is reduced significantly over that for a single entry system.

Readers who are not familiar with double entry bookkeeping should study a basic text on accounting in order to understand the difference between debits and credits and how they are used in recording financial transactions.

2. It should be a cash accounting system or a modified cash accrual system.

Sophisticated business accounting systems are all generally accrual basis systems. A family's checkbook accounting system or tax record keeping system is generally always a cash system.

In a cash system the only entries ever made are recorded when cash is received or spent. Financial statements reflect only those transactions that have occurred through the receipt or payment of cash.

In an accrual system not only are the cash transactions recorded but any commitments incurred which have not yet been paid, or income promised but not yet received, are recorded and reflected in the financial statements. In addition, certain assets paid for in advance or payments on account received in advance are adjusted to reflect that which has been actually used or earned. Depreciation may also be recorded.

For most congregations, the cash system is generally sufficient to report accurately the financial status of the congregation. However, some congregational treasurers will, in fact, adjust their records on a monthly and/or annual basis to reflect certain commitments not yet evidenced by a cash transaction.

Thus, bills which are due but not yet paid, such as for utilities, are recorded as an expense and as a liability of the congregation before being paid. Sometimes pledges which have been made to the congregation but not yet received are recorded as income and as a receivable. Again, for further clarification on how accruals are entered into the records, interested readers should refer to an accounting textbook.

3. It should be a fund accounting system.

Nonprofit organizations and governmental units generally use what is called a fund accounting approach to record keeping. Fund accounting differs from other types of accounting systems in that it separates into specific funds various aspects of the congregation's finances. A business corporation's system is intended to reflect a profit or loss in the operations. It is a one fund operation.

But nonprofit groups, such as congregations, generally receive and use cash contributions for current operations (current unrestricted fund), for buildings (building fund), to accumulate capital (capital funds), the income to be used for designated purposes (endowment fund), and for special purposes (restricted current funds). Better control over cash, more intelligible reporting, and a better stewardship of the congregation's cash resources are all advantages in using fund accounting.

However, a fund accounting system can be complicated bookkeeping even in the smallest operation. Many more entries are generally required if there are transfers between funds. Financial statement preparation may be more difficult and, in general, the system is difficult to maintain for inexperienced church bookkeepers.

But fund accounting is proper for congregations and should be the system used. The new AICPA accounting principles guide for nonprofit organizations suggests only fund accounting financial statements. A text on fund accounting should be referred to for more information on the mechanics of using fund accounting for congregations. (See the bibliography on pages 39-40.)

Just as certain concepts are basic to any church accounting system, certain accounting procedures are basic to any type of accounting system, whether fund accounting or something else. And congregational treasurers need to know the basic mechanics for keeping a set of church financial records. After all, church cash can be controlled only as leaders know how much cash there is or may be expected.

Journals and Ledgers

Any accounting system has certain basic tools used to analyze the flow of funds from receipts to payout.

1. A cash receipts journal (Illustration 4, p. 19) chronicles all cash received by date, month, year, source, and by purpose. As the offering is counted, for example, it is distributed to various funds for purposes designated by the donors. The information is recorded, totaled, and summarized by account. Totals are posted to ledger account balances.

ILLUSTRATION 4

Cash Receipts Journal
(Totals to be posted to General Ledger)

Date	Source	Deposit	Current Fund	Building Fund	Benevolences	Memorial Fund	Other
2/1	Offerings	600	500	100			
2/8	✓	500	300	100	100		
2/15	✓	700	600	50		50	
2/22	✓	500	400	50	50		
TOTALS		2300	1800	300	150	50	

19

ILLUSTRATION 5

Cash Disbursements Journal

(Totals to be posted to General Ledger)

Date	Payee	Check No.	Amount	Benevolences	Salaries	Utilities	Supplies	Debt Payments	Other
2/15	Utility Co	103	200			200			
2/20	Insurance	104	100						100
2/25	District Office	105	500	500					
2/28	Pastor Smith	106	1000		1000				
2/29	Book Store	107	50				50		
	TOTALS		1850	500	1000	200	50		100

ILLUSTRATION 6

Selected General Ledger Accounts
(Postings from Journals)

Date	Cash	J	Dr.	Cr.	Balance Dr.	Balance Cr.
	Balance Fund				200	
2/28		CR	2300		2500	
2/28		CD		1850	650	

Date	Offerings—Current	J	Dr.	Cr.	Balance Dr.	Balance Cr.
1/31		CR		1500		1500
2/28		CR		1800		3300

Date	Expense—Utilities	J	Dr.	Cr.	Balance Dr.	Balance Cr.
1/31		CD	300		300	
2/28		CD	200		500	

Date	Expense—Benevolences	J	Dr.	Cr.	Balance Dr.	Balance Cr.
1/31		CD	500		500	
2/28		CD	500		1000	

2. A cash disbursements journal (Illustration 5, page 20) lists all money spent in order of payout. Since prenumbered checks are used, they are listed in numerical order and allocated to the proper account and fund. Since expenses are paid by check (petty cash funds are another matter), each payment for goods or services is listed in the cash disbursements journal. A quick glance through the pages of a cash disbursements journal will reveal every payment made by the church treasurer.

Periodically, the columns are totaled to summarize various types of expenditures. The total of all account, or fund, columns must equal the total of the checks paid out as listed in the journal.

3. A general ledger (Illustration 6, page 21) provides information on the current balances of all accounts. Income and expense are summarized by accounts each period and then transferred (posted) to a specific general ledger account. Thus, a bookkeeper can know at anytime the total spent for the period on utilities, or rent, or supplies. The current cumulative costs for all assets, the net amount of cash on hand, and any liabilities are also available at a glance in the general ledger.

Financial statements are prepared from the account balances listed in the general ledger.

In addition, certain other subsidiary journals or ledgers can be developed. For example, individual member contribution records are listed in a separate ledger. The total of all contributions should be the same as the amount shown in the appropriate general ledger income account. A payroll journal will detail salaries paid and any amounts withheld for taxes or insurance, with the total paid being the same as total salary expense shown in the general ledger.

Bank Statement Reconciliation

A bank reconciliation form and procedure is an important part of the cash verification process for any organization with a checking account. The books of original entry (the journals) or final entry (ledgers) have no relationship to a bank reconciliation except, again, as verification that the cash balances shown in the general ledger (after posting from the journals) are accurate compared to the bank statement.

Reconciling the cash balances to what the bank statement reports is an important step in the bookkeeping function. After all, it is important to know just how much cash the congregation really has. Good church cash management must know that. Has the bank made any charge for services not recorded by the congregation? Are there missing deposits? Which checks have not yet cleared the bank? A bank reconciliation procedure is the only way to find out answers to these and other questions about the true amount of cash available to pay bills, or invest, or commit to another project.

Specific steps are involved in a bank reconciliation (these steps are also applicable to your personal checking account).

1. Determine which checks have not yet cleared the bank account. These are checks written by the congregational treasurer, subtracted from the congregation's records, but which have not yet cleared the bank, thus, not yet been deducted from the congregation's bank account balance. These are outstanding checks, which so far as the bank is concerned, are still cash belonging to the congregation.

2. Determine if all deposits recorded on the congregation's cash account have been recorded on the bank statement. Some may not be, particularly those made after the bank statement was prepared.

3. Determine from the bank statements if there are any changes or additions which the bank has made but which have not yet been made on the congregation's records. These may be bank service charges, bad checks written by members, or interest earned on the account (possible in some states).

4. Determine the cash balance on the bank statement. Add any deposits made but not yet recorded. Deduct all outstanding checks.

5. Determine the cash balance in the ledger. Deduct all bank charges, add any credits. The adjusted totals of the bank statement and the ledger should now be equal. If not, there may be an error some place. A check must be made to determine the cause of the difference.

For good church cash management the importance of a prompt bank reconciliation preparation cannot be overemphasized. It is the best way to verify that the cash expected to be available is available.

The Financial Statements

The sum of all debit account balances in the ledger must equal the sum of all credit account balances in the ledger. This is generally determined by preparing a trial balance, which is a listing of all accounts and their balances.

A work sheet (Illustration 7, page 24) is used, to tabulate the trial balance, make adjustments, if any, and to segregate accounts for purposes of financial statement preparation (Illustration 8, page 25).

The Cash Flow Forecast

Efficient church cash management is simply impossible without an adequate cash flow budget and analysis. Unless a congregation can anticipate its cash needs in the next month, months, or years, an effective utilization of cash resources will be difficult to achieve. By being able to anticipate when cash will be needed to pay for expenses and when cash will be available from offerings, a congregation can either invest surplus cash or attempt to rearrange large costs to avoid borrowings.

ILLUSTRATION 7

Trial Balance and Work Sheet

Accounts	Trial Balance YTD from GL		Adjustments		Adjusted Trial Balance		Closing Journal Entry		Final Trial Balance	
	Dr.	Cr.	Dr.	Cr.	Dr.	Cr.	Dr.	Cr.	Dr.	Cr.
Petty Cash	100				100				100	
Checking	650				650				650	
Savings Acct	5000				5000				5000	
Building or Eq	100,000				100,000				100,000	
Accounts Payable		-0-		① 400		400				400
Mortgages Payable		75000				75000				75000
Current Offering		3300				3300	3300			
Building Fund		700				700	700			
Benevolences		300				300	300			
Memorial		50				50	50			
Other		400				400	400			
Benevolences Exp	1000				1000			1000		
Salaries	2000				2000			2000		
Utilities	500		① 400		900			900		
Supplies	150				150			150		
Repairs	-0-				-0-			-0-		
Committees	500				505			500		
Other	500				500			500		
Fund Balance		30,650				30,650	300			30,350
① Unpaid Utility Bill										
TOTALS	110,400	110,400	400	400	110,800	110,800	5050	5050	105,750	105,750

24

ILLUSTRATION 8

Financial Statements

Balance Sheet (all funds combined)

Assets (at cost):		Liabilities:	
Cash—Checking account	$ 1,000	Accounts Payable	$ 400
Savings accounts	4,750	Mortgages Payable—	
Land	10,000	Church Building	50,000
Buildings—Church	50,000	Parsonage	25,000
Parsonage	30,000	Fund Balances:	
Equipment	10,000	General Operating Fund	1,350
	$105,750	Plant Fund	25,000
		Endowment Fund	4,000
			$105,750

Operating Statement

Income:	This Month	Year-to-Date	Budget-YTD
Current	$1800	$3300	$3500
Building Fund	300	700	1000
Benevolences	150	300	1000
Memorial Fund	50	50	–0–
Other	–0–	400	–0–
	$2300	$4750	$5500
Expenses:			
Benevolences	$ 500	$1000	$1000
Salaries	1000	2000	2000
Utilities	200	900	400
Supplies	50	150	50
Repairs	–0–	–0–	50
Committees	–0–	500	250
Other	100	500	1000
	$1850	$5050	$4750
Net change	$ 450	$ (300)	$ 750

In many congregations the use of a cash flow forecast will seem quite undramatic. The short term investments will usually generate a modest income. But the dampening of false euphoria in times of surplus and the advance notice of a shortfall of income provide a steadier, less emotion-filled point of view than one without forecast. Responsible planning takes on a new dimension with the use of cash flow forecasting.

Based on past experiences and a reasonably accurate budget (see the booklet, *Annual Budgeting*, in this series), a congregation can prepare a cash forecast worksheet without too much difficulty. (Note the format of Illustration 9, page 28.)

A monthly analysis of available cash will give a good picture of the ups and downs in cash needs during the year. Budget makers try to arrange expenses in such a way that high costs occur in months of substantial cash flow, and minimal costs are paid in low income months. Of course, some expenses are the same all year, but a few, such as insurance premiums, special purchases, and church school supplies can probably be paid for in the high income months.

Using a cash flow forecast will also permit a more advantageous scheduling of major renovations, purchases, and timely investments. If the forecasts project a substantial amount accumulating, say within the next eighteen months, and a new heating plant is needed for the church building, plans can be initiated now for installation of the equipment then. In the meantime, those surplus funds can be invested anticipating their eventual use for this specific project. Just waiting until the day "whenever funds will be available," not knowing when that may be, may delay the purchase beyond a reasonable time or even make it appear to be impossible. Doing nothing could be disastrous to the building's maintenance.

If a serious cash forecast reveals that eighteen months hence there is simply not going to be enough money available to continue the congregation's day care center, a planned cancellation of the service can be initiated rather than a sudden withdrawal of support and closing of the school.

Cash forecasting helps, among other things, to anticipate available cash and facilitates program planning.

Maximizing Cash Through Proper Spending

Church cash management is more than worrying about investing surplus cash or forecasting cash needs, it also involves careful use of purchasing and spending procedures. Congregations can "make money" by the way in which they spend their money. Purchasing controls and procedures are important for utilizing efficiently the cash resources available to a congregation.

To maximize a congregation's cash resources through better spending, therefore, requires development of some kind of controlled system for purchasing, that is, for spending the congregation's money. A system may be nothing more than the back side of a used mailer or envelope in the hip pocket of the pastor. It may be an elaborate system of signatures and countersignatures, computer calculations, and endless reams of forms. Between those extremes there should be a system useful to your congregation. Two charts which suggest ways of monitoring cash flow from offering to disbursement appear on pages 29 and 30.

Other booklets in this series will suggest appropriate purchasing procedures, but the procedure is important if a congregation expects to acquire "the right thing, in the right quality, in the right quantity, at the right time, at the right price, from the right vendor . . ." *

For example, if every church school teacher goes out to buy crayons individually for a class, it will cost the congregation much more than if someone bought a quantity supply and distributed crayons as needed to the teachers.

Or if some zealous member of the property committee went out to buy a lawn mower for the congregation's postage-stamp-sized lawn, it would be ridiculous to get a riding mower, or even a self propelled mower. It might not even make sense to buy a mower at all. A small lawn could be mowed with a borrowed mower.

Or if the pastor got a bargain on 100 reams of mimeograph paper, and only 20 are needed annually, the bargain might turn out to be expensive if the paper yellowed long before it could be used.

Or if the congregation's air conditioning system fails and the local dealer quotes a price but there is a big bargain in the town thirty miles down the road for a replacement system, that bargain might not make the most sense if that dealer can't or won't come that far to service the unit.

Yes, a purchasing system is important for management of the congregation's resources. If the congregation does not presently have a system, the time may have come to adopt one.

---

* From *The Art of Purchasing* by A. L. MacMillan. Copyright 1959 by A. L. MacMillan. Reprinted by permission of Exposition Press Inc., Hicksville, NY 11801.

ILLUSTRATION 9

Cash Forecast Worksheet

Revenues Expected

	Total	Jan.	Feb.	Mar.	Apr.	May	June	July	Aug.	Sept.	Oct.	Nov.	Dec.
Offerings	36000	3000	3500	4000	3000	3000	2500	2000	1500	3000	3000	3500	4000
Interest	800			200			200			200			200
Rentals	900	100	100	100	100	100				100	100	100	100
Specials	800			300									500
Etc.	2300	200	200	200	200	100	100	100	100	200	200	300	400
Total	40800	3300	3800	4800	3300	3200	2800	2100	1600	3500	3300	3900	5200

Disbursements Planned Budget

	Total	Jan.	Feb.	Mar.	Apr.	May	June	July	Aug.	Sept.	Oct.	Nov.	Dec.
Benevolences	3600	300	300	300	300	300	300	300	300	300	300	300	300
Salaries	18000	1500	1500	1500	1500	1500	1500	1500	1500	1500	1500	1500	1500
Expenses	12350	1200	1300	1000	1650	800	600	600	800	1000	1100	1100	1200
Debt payments	6000	500	500	500	500	500	500	500	500	500	500	500	500
Etc.	850	100	100	50	50					100	150	200	100
Total	40800	3600	3700	3350	4000	3100	2900	2900	3100	3400	3550	3600	3600
Difference	0	(300)	100	1450	(700)	100	(100)	(800)	(1500)	100	(250)	300	1600

ILLUSTRATION 10

Flow Chart - Offerings

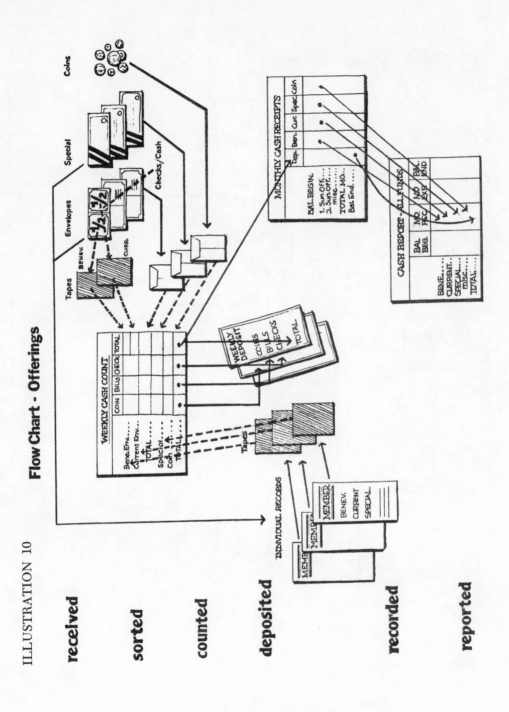

received

sorted

counted

deposited

recorded

reported

Reprinted by permission from the book,
Complete Handbook of Church Accounting,
by Holck and Holck. Copyright © 1978 by
Prentice-Hall, Inc. Englewood Cliffs, N.J.

ILLUSTRATION 11

Flow Chart - Disbursements

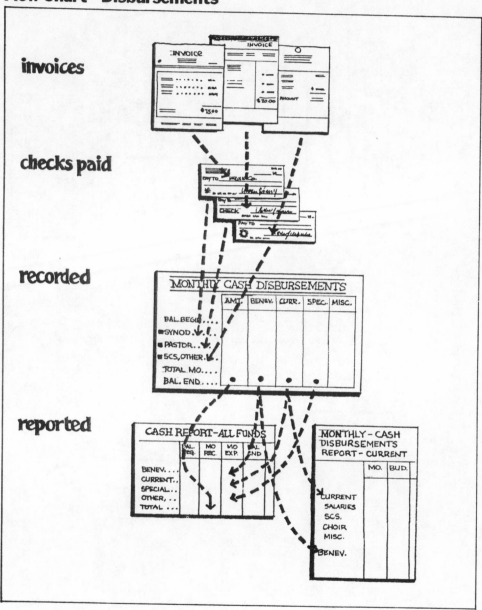

How to
invest
surplus cash

Church cash management includes not only the safeguarding of money, it also involves the careful use of that money. Therefore, earning interest on surplus money is not all there is to cash management, although it is a very important part. How money is used for investing is equally as important as how money is spent.

Available cash must be managed and the techniques for managing that cash will vary from congregation to congregation. Nevertheless, all money managers, those who invest cash for clients or for their own account, use certain techniques to maximize the return or yield on the cash invested. Cash management by investment is predicated on the principle of investing cash to get more money to invest to get even more money. The wisest stewardship of congregational resources would insist that cash be put to its best use. Cash can be invested several ways for the benefit of the congregation.

Investment Vehicles for Cash

Many congregations find that the typical savings and loan association's daily interest savings account gives the most flexibility to investing surplus cash with a yield consistent with the safety of such funds. Minimum interest rates are currently 5¼% (1977) but they do fluctuate. For funds that may not be invested for a long period or which must be available on short notice, the daily interest account offers a real opportunity.

Here's how such an account can be used to maximum advantage by a congregation. Instead of depositing the Sunday offering into the congregation's checking account, the deposit could be made directly to a savings account. The same analysis of the offering must be retained as before, but whether the cash goes to savings or checking makes no difference. Then, whenever money is needed to write checks sufficient cash can be transferred from savings to checking.

The procedure keeps idle cash out of the checking account until it is needed. In many places such transfers can be made by telephone.

Such an account could prove extremely worthwhile for some congregations. $1,000 will earn 14¢ a day in a 5¼% daily deposit account. That may not seem like much, but for some congregations the sum could add a few hundred dollars a year to their program.

In states where NOW (Negotiable Order of Withdrawal) accounts are available, checking accounts already earn interest. The use of a daily passbook account would seem unnecessary then in order to keep surplus cash earning interest.

Cash that may not be needed for a longer period of time could be put into certificates of deposit at a local savings and loan association. The yield is higher, but the congregation commits itself to a longer investment time, too. Although the cash is readily available any time, a substantial penalty is imposed on early withdrawals.

Cash invested in most savings and loan associations is insured up to $40,000 through the Federal Savings and Loan Insurance Corporation, an agency of the federal government. Most checking accounts, also, are insured by the Federal Deposit Insurance Corporation for up to $40,000.

A Word of Caution

It is possible for congregations to invest their cash in other places and perhaps receive a greater yield. But the money in such instances may not be insured and the risk of loss is greatly increased. Yet, for higher yields, some congregations may want to consider the possibility. In such cases it will be important to secure advice from the congregation's bank or a trusted investment counselor.

It is important that congregational leaders maintain a very cautious approach to any investment of the congregation's money. After all, that money was given for a specific purpose. It is managed in trust for the donors by the church council for the benefit of recipients. Negligent use of funds could precipitate a suit against congregational leaders. Even if no suit results, the loss of trust can be traumatic.

Thus, while an individual or a business may invest in certain high risk ventures, congregations have no business risking money given to them in dubious enterprises offering unrealistically promised yields. A cautious, conservative approach is generally both prudent and responsible. While not as much money may be earned, it won't be lost on some high flyer.

Nevertheless, there are other vehicles than savings accounts for investing church cash. Government securities are safe, of course, and savings bonds earn a respectable 6%, both Series E and H. Yields on Treasury bills are sometimes low, but the investment is safe. For three or more months available investment time, these bills offer another opportunity.

It makes no sense, however, for a church or other nonprofit organization to invest in tax exempt municipal securities when higher yields can be obtained elsewhere. Tax exempt municipals are not insured and in addition are a more natural choice for individual taxpayers in high tax brackets.

Money market mutual funds offer an opportunity for cash investment at savings accounts yields or more. These are funds that use money received from investors to purchase $100,000 blocks of commercial paper. By participating in a money market fund, an individual investor can get the advantage of the yield on larger minimum investments, with only a small personal investment. But, money market funds are not insured. Risk of loss of principle, however, is small.

Surplus congregational cash should never be invested in common stocks, and probably not in commercial bonds, either. Even putting the congregation's endowment fund into stocks and bonds exposes it to a severe potential loss of capital in a falling market. A careful analysis of such investment areas should be made prior to their use. It is often better stewardship to stick with a savings account.

Special Funds and Their Investment

Congregations may have cash available from several sources for investment—current fund surpluses, building funds, etc. Thus, depending on the urgency for use of such funds, various types of investments are possible.

The current fund most likely to be available for short-term investing would be surplus current operating cash. At peak offering times in the church year, extra cash should be put to work in a savings account, and then withdrawn when needed.

Endowment funds are generally rather permanent investments. Thus long term commitments can be made, but they must be safe and prudent. Four year certificates in a savings and loan offer a possibility with good yields. Income from endowment funds is generally used to supplement the current budget, or to fund special projects.

Congregations often accumulate funds in a building fund anticipating the time when they have enough money available to build a building. While waiting for the fund to accumulate, the cash should be safely invested. Again, certificates of deposit at a savings and loan association offer a reasonable return for stated periods of time, safely insured without risk of loss. Government securities, such as treasury bills, would offer equal protection, but perhaps less yield. Stocks and bonds are to be avoided.

If a congregation has a sinking fund required to pay off the indebtedness on a church building, care must be exercised to invest those funds in such places where principal is preserved intact, liquidity is assured, and the investment vehicle is not in violation of the sinking fund trust agreement. Here local professional advice, which can be informed about state laws, will be invaluable.

For the short term, cash is managed by putting it in those investment vehicles deemed best for the purpose. For the long term, availability of cash and cash use must be carefully planned. Cash management involves the current use or investing of cash; cash planning anticipates the use or investment of cash for the longer term. Effective church cash management involves both present and future planning through the use of investment vehicles and skillful budgeting for spending.

Specific procedures for cash investment can be ascertained from the offices of a bank or a savings and loan association. Descriptive literature abounds. The prudent church leader will be cautious in selection of a vehicle, using that method that provides the highest yield consistent with safety and the preservation of capital.

Interfund Borrowings

Congregations often develop surplus cash in one fund, such as a building fund, but incur deficits in other funds, such as the current operating fund, thus presenting a tempting dilemma. The question is whether to use surplus cash in the building fund to pay the utility bills and the pastor's salary.

Too often, unwise decisions are made, and more problems occur. The easy solution of course is to borrow (temporarily, of course) from the building fund to meet the current fund crisis. But if the current fund is always going to have a crisis, is always borrowing from the building fund, neither the current fund problem will be solved nor a building built.

Effective church management techniques suggest that interfund borrowing is dangerous. It is simply too easy never to repay. The congregation should invest its building fund cash in a prudent manner with others and then, if necessary, go out to borrow funds to cover the deficit.

The pressure of repayment will force some serious thinking on congregational leaders about ways to reduce spending, raise more money, and pay off that debt. Simply borrowing from the building fund will never generate that demand. Inter-fund borrowings are possible. They often occur. But they can be a dangerous sign of ineffective leadership and poor church cash management.

Other Cash Management Opportunities

Congregations may be the recipients of cash to be managed as a foundation, trust funds, memorials, or grant. Each of these would have a specific purpose or eventual use, presumably to the benefit of the congregation. Until the cash is available for use of the program, it is to be invested and managed as carefully as possible. Previous suggestions on yield, liquidity, safety, and risk are applicable for these funds, too. Professional counsel may be needed to avoid inadvertent conflict with federal or state laws if a foundation is created.

When the church is the recipient of a deferred giving contract, a living trust, or even a sum for the establishment of an endowment fund, the principles and techniques of cash management outlined here are appropriate. Any restricted fund, such as these may be, that is limited as to use, or time of use, must be carefully managed.

Churches now come under new tax legislation which imposes a tax on the income earned that is so-called unrelated business income. In the management of a congregation's cash, church leaders must be careful to put cash to work without creating taxable income as well.

Income generated from sources other than the Sunday offering are generally not subject to income tax if the congregation[1]

1. Sells merchandise which has been donated versus merchandise which has been purchased or produced.

2. Uses unpaid volunteers (versus paid employees) when engaging in otherwise taxable activities.

3. Receives royalties versus the development of the property on its own initiative.

4. Avoids debt financed property, unless the property is clearly related to the exempt function, or unless it is real property covered by the 15-year rule[2].

---

[1] Malvern J. Gross, "Churches and the Tax on Unrelated Business Income," *The Philanthropy Monthly*, July 1976. Reprinted with permission of *The Philanthropy Monthly*.

[2] Ibid. "If the church acquired the property for future church use, and if that church use begins within 15 years of the acquisition of the property, then the rental income is not taxable, even if the property is debt financed." Gross, "Churches and the Tax on Unrelated Business Income."

Handling Benevolence Monies

Benevolence contributions are to be paid regularly for the purposes intended by the donor. Sometimes congregations use or hold such contributions for the purpose of making short term temporary investments to earn extra income or to meet current expense commitments, paying out the benevolences only at the last possible moment.

Some leaders may consider that good church cash management because it maximizes the return on that cash for the benefit of the congregation. Others would say that it is even good stewardship to accumulate that money for investments to earn more.

But benevolence monies are given for a purpose and a need that is generally immediate. Denominational budgets, hospitals, and other institutions depend on a steady flow of funds to finance their program. It may be smart money manipulation to hold such funds, but it is not good stewardship. In fact, it is neither good churchmanship nor good church cash management. When a gift is made for others, it should not be delayed, or it penalizes those to whom it is given.

In support
of the mission
of the church

There is no one best way to manage the cash funds of a congregation. There are many ways. The best ways are those that meet the immediate situation and need. Various basic rules and principles are applicable, but the variety of options available and of lay leaders responsible for a congregational cash management program make certain that no two congregations will ever do things exactly the same—nor should they. Each congregation has its own mission in the kingdom of God. A shared identity of concern does not mean identical ways of responding to its ministry.

The capacity of the leadership, the understanding of the membership, and the availability of cash will certainly also have an influence on how a congregation's cash is managed.

One thing is certain, however. No congregational leader should tolerate "lazy money." If there is any idle cash at all, a congregation can earn at least something on it. Even a few dollars can be put in a savings account, there to compound interest earnings at 5% or more. Good cash managers, whether at home, or in business, or in the church, put all their money to work. They maximize their resources in many ways, but among the best ways, they put their cash to work for them.

Good cash management is not only the process of investing money, as has been pointed out several times already in this volume. It is also the intelligent use of that money. And when lay leaders are perceived by the membership to be engaged in effective church cash management, there is confidence in their ability to handle the financial problems of the congregation as well as to make the most of the cash which the congregation does have.

Competent cash management fosters confidence in the ability of the lay leaders to meet the congregation's financial commitments. It enhances careful budget planning, sound spending habits, and the maximum use of resources.

Planning of any sort is intended to reach certain goals. Church cash management, done effectively, is a planning process that attempts to achieve certain financial goals, whether to balance the budget, make up a deficit, accumulate money for a building program, or raise funds for a special project, or to achieve specific congregational goals.

In all that is done, however, church cash management, as with any other facet of church management, aims to fulfill the mission of the church. It is no more or less than that task which prompts the writing of this booklet for the benefit of congregational leaders.

Bibliography

American Institute of Certified Public Accountants, "*A Tentative Set of Accounting Principles and Reporting Practices for Nonprofit Organizations Not Covered by Existing AICPA Industry Audit Guides.*" AICPA, 1211 Avenue of the Americas, New York, N.Y. 10036. 1977. This tentative draft is to be followed by a second draft in 1978. The title and date of the final publication had not been set when this book was published. When published, this document will be the standard document used by accountants for certain nonprofit organizations, including congregations and religious organizations.

Gray, Robert N. *Managing the Church* (Church Business Administration Vol. I, Business Methods Vol. II). Enid, Okla.: The Phillips University Press. 1971. (Dr. Gary Gray, FCBA, National Institute on Church Management, 8295 N.W. Barrybrooke Dr., Kansas City, MO 64151.) Volume I identifies the various functions or processes found in the managerial task as they relate to church management. Volume II deals with specific management techniques for personnel, public relations, cash control, accounting principles, insurance, property, etc.

Gross, Malvern, J. Jr. *Financial and Accounting Guide for Nonprofit Organizations*, 2nd ed. New York: Ronald Press. 1974. A financial management, accounting, and reporting guide for the nonaccountant treasurer or director of a nonprofit organization.

Gross, Malvern J. Jr. *The Layman's Guide to Preparing Financial Statements for Churches*. New York: American Institute of Certified Public Accountants, 1969. A concise description of financial statements preparation procedures—brief, yet extremely useful for treasurers of small and medium-sized congregations. Currently out of print. Libraries in some areas may still catalog it.

Holck, Manfred Jr., ed. *Church Management: The Clergy Journal*. Church Management, Inc., 4119 Terrace Lane, Hopkins, MN 55343. A professional magazine for clergy and church administrators. Topics include stewardship, finance, budgeting, accounting, personnel, taxes, buildings, sermons, and other church related subjects. Ten issues annually.

Holck, Manfred Jr., ed. *Church and Clergy Finance*. Ministers Life Resources, Minneapolis, MN. A professional semi-monthly financial newsletter for clergy, church treasurers, and lay leaders of congregations. Issues include information on church financial management.

Holck, Manfred Jr. and Holck, Manfred Sr., *Complete Handbook of Church Accounting*. Englewood Cliffs, New Jersey: Prentice-Hall, Inc. 1978. A comprehensive handbook on all aspects of church accounting. Includes discussions on fund accounting, accounting for cash, internal control, audits, and more. Many illustrations and sample financial statements.

Holck, Manfred Jr., *Money and Your Church*. New Canaan, Conn.: Keats Publishing, Inc. 1974. A popular handbook describing proven ways to raise more money for the local congregation and manage it better, too. Chapters include topics on fund raising, budgeting, purchasing, ministerial compensation, accounting, and more.

Lindgren, Alvin J. and Shawchuck, Norman. *Management for Your Church*. Nashville, TN, Abingdon 1977. Applying contemporary systems theory to the church institution, interaction to environment, program planning and budgeting, problem analysis, and decision analysis for pastors and lay leaders.

Montana, Patrick J. and Borst, Diane, *Managing Nonprofit Organizations*. New York: American Management Association. 1977. A useful handbook for better ways of managing nonprofit organizations, including congregations. Includes essays on planning and analysis, management by objectives, project management and participatory management, and more.

Walz, Edgar, *Church Business Methods: A Handbook for Pastors and Leaders of the Congregation*. St. Louis: Concordia. 1970. Suggested business procedures applicable to congregational financial record keeping.